HEINEMANN Profiles

Anne Frank

Richard Tames

Heinemann

First published in Great Britain by
Heinemann Library
Halley Court, Jordan Hill,
Oxford OX2 8EJ
a division of Reed Educational and
Professional Publishing Ltd.
Heinemann is a registered trademark of
Reed Educational & Professional
Publishing Limited.

OXFORD MELBOURNE
AUCKLAND KUALA LUMPUR
SINGAPORE IBADAN NAIROBI
KAMPALA JOHANNESBURG
GABORONE PORTSMOUTH NH
CHICAGO

Designed by Visual Image, Taunton.
Printed in Hong Kong / China

Details of written sources:
Anne Frank in the World, Anne Frank
Stichting, 1985; Gies, Miep, *Anne Frank
Remembered*, Bantam Press, 1987;
Manheim R and Mok M (trans), *Tales
from the Secret Annexe*, Penguin, 1986;
Marland M (ed), Goodrich F and Hackett
A, *The Diary of Anne Frank* (play), Blackie,
1970.

03 02
10 9 8 7 6 5 4 3

ISBN 0 431 08618 4

This title is also available in a hardback
library edition (ISBN 0 431 08611 7)

**British Library Cataloguing in
Publication Data**

Tames, Richard, 1946–
    Anne Frank. – (Heinemann Profiles)
    1.Frank, Anne, 1929–1945 – Juvenile
    literature 2.Holocaust, Jewish
    (1939–1945) – Juvenile literature
    I.Title
    940.5'3'088296

Acknowledgements
The Publishers would like to thank the
following for permission to reproduce
photographs: AKG Photo pp4, 5, 8, 14,
39; Anne Frank Stichting pp6, 15, 23, 26
(e, f, g), 32, 38; Benelux Press b.v. pp25, 26
(a, b, d, h), 28, 30; Chris Honeywell p49;
Historisches Museum, Frankfurt-am-
Main p11; Miep Gies p17; Popperfoto
pp26 (c), 44; Rijksintituut voor
Oologsdocumentatie pp18, 19, 37, 41;
Spaarnestad Fotoarchief pp10, 16, 20, 27,
31, 35, 36, 40, 42, 45; Topham
Picturepoint pp7, 47.

Cover photograph reproduced with
permission of Wiener Library

Any words appearing in the text in bold,
like this, are explained in the Glossary.

This book includes extracts from Anne Frank, *The Diary of a Young Girl
The Definitive Edition*, edited by Otto H. Frank and Mirjam Pressler,
translated by Susan Massotty, Penguin Books 1997.

CONTENTS

WHO WAS ANNE FRANK?

In 1933 the **Nazis** came to power in Germany. They began to **persecute** everyone they considered enemies or opponents. Highest on their list were Jews. By 1945, when the Second World War ended, at least 6,000,000 Jews, possibly more, would be dead – shot, gassed, beaten or worked to death. Others died of cold, hunger or disease. Anne Frank, herself born in Germany, was one of those millions. But, unlike most of those whose lives were so brutally cut short, her words still reach out from beyond her grave – wherever that may be.

Anne Frank in 1942 – the year she and her family went into hiding.

THE TEENAGER

Almost as soon as Anne Frank became a teenager she had to give up her friends, her pleasures and even her pet cat, to go into hiding from the Nazis. When she might have been going out dating and dancing she passed years in hiding, wishing the days away. She could see a world outside but never take part in it because for her it meant danger and death. She recorded her dreams and fears in the diary she called 'Kitty'. Kitty became the best friend she felt she had never had.

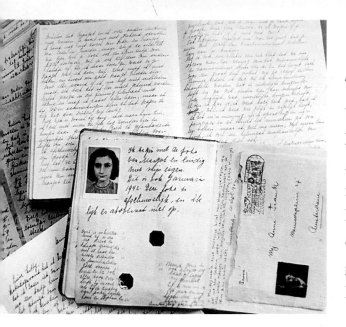

THE WRITER

Writing to Kitty passed long days but also helped Anne to examine her feelings and understand herself better. She decided that when she grew up she would earn her living as a writer.

Pages from Anne's diary – the picture in the diary is of Anne herself.

Unlike other writers, Anne Frank could only travel from one floor to another, and saw no-one but the same dozen people, day in, day out, from one year's end to the next. She lived like a prisoner but she fought to keep her mind free.

EPITAPH

Anne Frank's short life ended in squalor and misery, separated from all who had loved her. Anne dreamed that one day she would grow up to become a famous writer. She did become a famous writer, but never had the chance to grow up to be an adult.

Where Anne Frank lived and died.

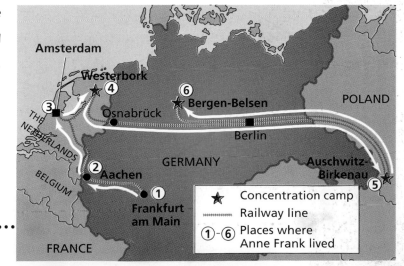

THE FRANK FAMILY

The Frank family first settled in the German city of Frankfurt-am-Main in the 17th century. Frankfurt grew rich on trade and finance and as the city prospered so did the Frank family. Anne Frank's grandfather was a banker. Her father, Otto, briefly studied art at university. At the age of 20 he decided to join a friend in America and work in the famous New York department store, Macy's. A year later Otto's father died. Otto went back to Germany and got a job in an engineering factory in the industrial city of Düsseldorf.

World War I broke out when Otto was 25. Both he and two of his brothers served in the army. Otto rose to the rank of lieutenant. After the war he went to work with the bank his father had worked for.

Anne Frank's father, Otto (right), served in the German army during World War I.

MARRIAGE AND A FAMILY

In 1925 Otto Frank married Edith Hollander, who came from Aachen in northern Germany, near the border with the Netherlands. Otto was by now quite well off, so they had a honeymoon in Italy. Then they settled in Frankfurt.

Otto Frank with his two daughters – Margot (left) and baby Anne,

For the first two years they lived with Otto's mother, before moving into a home of their own. Their first child, Margot Betti, was born in 1926. In 1929 they had a second daughter. They called her Annelies Marie – but Anne for short. Taking care of two small children kept Edith very busy but Otto was able to pay for a housemaid, Kathi, to help her. Otto was also a keen amateur photographer and took many pictures of his growing family.

THE GREAT CRASH

For people in business 1929 was a terrible year. The prosperity of the United States, the richest country in the world, suddenly collapsed. Many banks lost huge sums that they had loaned to businesses, so they were unable to pay people who had trusted them with their savings. Every country that did business with America was affected. Throughout Europe people rushed to take their savings out of banks. Factories closed down. Millions of people lost their jobs.

Queues of unemployed people in Germany. Notice the Hitler slogan and swastika on the wall of the building.

By 1932 the factories in Frankfurt were only making a third of the goods they had manufactured in 1929, and 70,000 of the city's residents were unemployed. One person in four had no regular income. Soup kitchens were opened to give out a basic meal to people living in poverty. People were frightened and angry and found it difficult to understand why things were going wrong.

MOVING ON

Otto Frank was lucky. He still had a job. He also had a happy family and a pleasant home in the suburbs. But in 1933 he decided to give up everything he had worked for and take his family to start all over again in a foreign country – the Netherlands. This was because 1933 was the year in which Adolf Hitler and the **Nazi** Party came to power in Germany. Hitler and the Nazis blamed Germany's problems on the Jews, many of whom were important in banking and other types of business.

Frankfurt had a Jewish population of 30,000, who accounted for just over one-twentieth of the city's population. Throughout Germany only Berlin had a larger Jewish community. The Frank family were part of Frankfurt's Jewish community. With the Nazis in power Otto swiftly decided that Germany – the country he had fought for in World War I – was no longer safe for him and his family.

THE RISE OF THE NAZIS

Germany was defeated in World War I. Although no enemy set foot on German land, its people were near starving, so the government gave up fighting. Many ordinary German soldiers believed they had been betrayed, not beaten, and were furious. One of those soldiers was Adolf Hitler.

HITLER, ARYANS AND JEWS

Hitler was not born in Germany but in Austria. As a young man he dreamed of becoming a great artist but he was lazy and ended up living little better than a tramp. Hitler began to develop ideas about why the world had failed to make him a success.

Nazis parade the streets with notices saying 'Germans! Beware! Don't buy from Jews.'

He believed that people could be divided into different races and that conflict between races was the key to history. Hitler declared that the most superior people were the Aryans of northern Europe, who ought to be united as a single nation and rule the whole world. Other races, such as the Slavs of eastern Europe (Russians, Poles and others), Asians, Africans and especially Jews, ought to work as slaves for the Aryans until they died out altogether.

As Nazis take over the local town hall in Frankfurt, a German crowd gives the Nazi salute. Notice the Nazi **swastika** flag on the balcony.

The Nazis emerge

During World War I Hitler joined the German army, won two medals for bravery and enjoyed army life. Hitler blamed the Jews for Germany's defeat. He said they only wanted to make money and cared nothing for Germany. This completely ignored the fact that many Jews, like Otto Frank and his brothers, had served bravely in the army during the war.

In 1919 Hitler joined a small new political group – the National Socialist German Workers' Party – Nazis for short. He soon became its leader, promising to make Germany the greatest country in the world. The Nazis had their own private army, the **SA** (*Sturmabteilungen*, Stormtroopers) to beat up their opponents, especially **communists**. The parades and uniforms appealed to many unemployed ex-soldiers.

The morning after 'Kristallnacht' – The windows of a Jewish-owned shop have been smashed by a Nazi mob.

THE NAZIS IN POWER

When the Great Crash of 1929 threw the country into crisis more and more people began to listen to Hitler. He promised to lead Germany to a bright future. In 1933 Hitler finally became head of government. Within months he began to make himself a **dictator** and started to **persecute** Germany's Jews.

On 1 April 1933, Germans were told by the new Nazi government that they should not buy goods in shops owned by Jews or use the services of Jewish doctors and lawyers. Jews were not allowed to be teachers either. By the end of 1933, 150,000 people opposed to the Nazis had been arrested and sent to **concentration camps**. In 1935 marriage between **Aryans** and Jews was made illegal.

Between 9 and 11 November 1938, dozens of **synagogues** and thousands of Jewish shops were smashed up and set on fire by mobs. The police did nothing. This nationwide riot was known as '*Kristallnacht*' (the night of breaking glass). The following day 30,000 Jewish men and boys were arrested and sent to concentration camps. Many Jews realized that things were only going to get worse and that they had to escape. By the spring of 1939 half of Germany's 500,000 Jews had left the country. Meanwhile Hitler continued to prepare for a war to put all of Europe under German leadership.

A New Home in a New Country

Otto Frank chose to take his family to the Netherlands because it had a long history of welcoming foreigners. Amsterdam, the biggest city, had a large Jewish community. During World War I the Netherlands had been **neutral**, taking no part in the fighting. A peaceful, prosperous, neighbouring country seemed like a safe place for the family. Of course, they would have to speak Dutch, but the children were young and would learn easily.

Moving by stages

In 1933 Mrs Frank took Margot and Anne with her to Aachen, near the Dutch border, to live with her mother, while Mr Frank went ahead to Amsterdam. He had to find a new home and start up a new business. The business was a branch of a German company called Opekta which made pectin, a

The Frank family on the way to the wedding of Otto's secretary, Miep Gies.

Anne (arrowed) in class at her new Dutch school.

substance used to make jams and jellies set solid. Edith and Margot joined him in December 1933. Anne joined them in February 1934, once their new home was fully furnished.

GETTING ON WELL

The Frank family home was in a bright, new suburb. It was a third-floor apartment, looking out on to a green. It had a flat roof at the back for sunbathing in warm weather. As more new homes were built round about, other families moved in and the children soon had many friends – Jewish, Catholic and Protestant. There was little motor traffic, so it was safe to play in the streets. Margot and Anne could go shopping or to the cinema in the city centre with their mother, and the seaside was not far away.

A new home in a new district – the Franks lived in a large housing block, looking out on to a green, newly planted with trees and shrubs.

Of course, the girls also had to go to school. They were both soon getting very good reports but Anne was a great chatterbox and often had to do extra homework as a punishment for talking when she should have been paying attention.

Anne was often cross with her older sister because Margot was praised by her parents for being quiet and tidy and taking good care of her clothes. Anne's favourite interests were pets, film stars, Greek myths, riding her bicycle and going to a local ice-cream parlour called Oasis.

Mr. Frank's business did so well that he had to hire new staff. One of them, Miep Santrouschitz, was an Austrian who became a close family friend. Later she married a Dutchman, Jan Gies, and became Mrs Miep Gies.

In 1938 Mr Frank started a second company, to sell herbs for seasoning meat. His partner in the new venture was Mr van Daan, another Jewish businessman, who had also left his home in Germany, bringing his wife and son, Peter, with him.

DANGER AHEAD?

Mr Frank continued to worry about the news from Germany, where conditions became worse and worse for Jews. In 1938 Mrs Frank's two brothers managed to get away to America. Her mother came to live in the Netherlands.

Otto Frank with his secretary Miep, who would later bring the Frank family their food when they were in hiding.

Britain, France and Germany seemed almost ready to go to war with each other that year but the crisis passed. In 1939 Britain and France finally did go to war with Germany when it invaded Poland. But the Netherlands was expected to remain **neutral** again and stay out of the fighting.

CONQUERED!

INVASION

On 10 May 1940 Germany invaded the Netherlands without warning, taking the Dutch armed forces completely by surprise. The Dutch Royal Family and government fled to Britain. German bombers raided the port of Rotterdam, destroying over 24,000 houses and killing almost 1000 people. By 15 May the Netherlands was under German control.

NEW RULERS, NEW RULES

Dutch people soon found that everyone had to carry an identity card and that their food was rationed.

German paratroops invade the Netherlands. The speed and power of the German forces ended the fighting in a matter of days.

BOSBAD

Herinnering Nederland 10 Mei 19

Life was to be far worse for the 140,000 Jews in the Netherlands. In October 1940 all Jewish businesses were required to register with the German authorities. Mr Frank realized that this meant that the Germans were planning to take them over. So he transferred his business to the name of trusted Dutch friends.

All Jews, adults and children, were forced to wear a yellow star with the word 'Jew' on it.

In June 1941 all Jews had the letter 'J' stamped on their identity card so that they could be picked out more easily. In September 1941 Margot and Anne were forced to leave their school and go to a separate school, where there were only Jewish pupils and teachers.

German troops arresting people suspected of wanting to fight back. Most would be imprisoned and many shot. Often their families never knew what had happened to them.

A PEOPLE APART

From May 1942 onwards all Jews over the age of six had to wear on their clothes a yellow Star of David badge with the word 'Jew' on it. This meant any Jew could be instantly identified on sight. Many people feared that even being seen talking to a Jewish friend or neighbour would mean trouble.

Jews were banned from trams and forbidden to own cars or even bicycles. All their shopping had to be done between three and five in the afternoon and only in special Jewish shops. Jews had to stay indoors from eight each evening until six the next morning. They had to get their hair cut only at a Jewish barber-shop. They were banned from using public swimming-pools.

ROUND-UPS AND RESISTANCE

In February 1941 street-fights broke out between Dutch **Nazis** and Dutch Jews. After a Dutch Nazi was killed, German troops surrounded the main Jewish neighbourhood and rounded up 400 Jewish men and boys. They were arrested and taken away – no-one knew where.

Many Dutch people protested by joining a two-day strike. Later, resistance would become more organized. Dutch people learned to forge official cards and permits, destroy records and files. They printed secret newsletters about the progress of the war. They got their information from BBC radio broadcasts from Britain.

Unemployed Dutchmen were also rounded up and sent to work in Germany where there was a shortage of men because so many Germans were in the armed forces. In January 1942 chosen Jewish families were ordered to report to Westerbork, a camp in the eastern Netherlands, from where they would be sent on to work elsewhere. Many Jews feared that they were being sent to work as slave labour and decided to go into hiding. Mr Frank began to work patiently, making careful preparations for his family and the van Daans to do just that.

The Secret Annexe

Mr Frank spent months getting ready for hiding. Clothes, furniture and food were sent to friends to prevent the Germans seizing them. Bedding, tables and chairs, 150 tins of vegetables and 30 kilograms of dried peas and beans were secretly smuggled into Mr Frank's warehouse and office at 263 Prinsengracht. On Monday 29 June 1942 Dutch newspapers carried a notice that all Jews would be sent to work in Germany. That week Otto Frank finally told Anne about his preparations. She was very surprised.

The Secret Annexe occupied rooms at the rear of the second and third floors of 263 Prinsengracht and could not be seen directly from the front of the building.

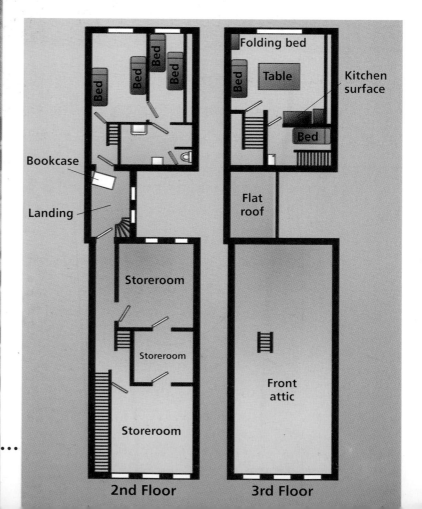

Bookcase

Landing

Bed
Bed
Bed
Bed

Folding bed

Table

Kitchen surface

Bed

Bed

Flat roof

Storeroom

Storeroom

Front attic

Storeroom

2nd Floor

3rd Floor

Doorway to safety – how the entrance to the secret annexe was disguised.

Later that same day Anne was even more surprised when an official letter was delivered, ordering Margot to report to the camp at Westerbork. That decided it. The Franks and the van Daans decided to go into hiding the very next day.

PACKING

Anne put her most precious things in her school satchel, starting with the diary she had been given a few weeks before, on her thirteenth birthday. She added 'hair-curlers, handkerchiefs, school books, a comb, old letters; I put in the craziest things … But I'm not sorry, memories mean more to me than dresses.' (Diary entry, 8 July 1942, p20)

The family signed a postcard to Mr Frank's sister, who was safe, like his mother, in **neutra**l Switzerland. Obviously they dared not say what they were going to do, so the message simply said, rather mysteriously: 'It is a pity that we can no longer correspond with you, but that is how it is. You must understand.'

Miep came round with her husband twice that day and carried away bags of clothes. Even so, when the family left their apartment early the next morning, they piled on all the clothes they could.

SETTLING IN

The Franks' home was four kilometres from Prinsengracht. As Jews were forbidden to use any form of transport they just had to walk all the way, carrying shopping-bags stuffed with possessions. It was probably fortunate that it was pouring with rain because they would have looked strangely over-dressed if it had been a bright summer's day. When they arrived there was a lot of sorting-out to do.

'All day long we unpacked boxes, filled cupboards, hammered nails and tidied up the mess, until we fell exhausted into our clean beds….' (10 July 1942, p25)

24

At first Anne found the hiding-place exciting – 'like being on holiday in a very strange **pension**.' (11 July 1942, p26) But a holiday is a time for going out, playing and having fun. Anne had to learn to sit still for hours at a time. No noisy chattering now because it might be heard outside.

The Franks were a loving and happy family but, cooped up together, they soon began to find daily life difficult. Mr and Mrs Frank hated the nearby church clock, which chimed every fifteen minutes, day and night. At night Margot's coughing woke Anne up. A week after the Franks moved into the secret annexe they were joined by Mr and Mrs van Daan and their teenage son, Peter. So everyone was even more confined. And Mrs van Daan soon made it clear that she found Anne a tiresome nuisance.

The room shared by Anne and Margot. They put up pictures and postcards to brighten up the walls.

THE DAILY ROUTINE

In November 1942 the seven people in the annexe were joined by an eighth, Mr Dussel. Mr Frank thought there was no more risk in hiding eight than seven and it would mean one more safe from the **Nazis**. Besides, Mr Dussel was a dentist, which might be very useful as no-one with a tooth ache could go out for treatment.

With eight people living in six rooms daily life had to be carefully organized.

In hiding: the eight people confined together in the annexe were a) Mr Frank b) Mrs Frank c) Anne d) Margot e) Mr van Daan f) Mr Dussel g) Mrs van Daan h) Peter van Daan.

Otto Frank's office building at 263 Prinsengracht. The door on the far left led up to the annexe, the middle door to the second floor office and the door on the right led to the ground floor warehouse.

MORNING

The alarm clock rang at 6.45 am each morning. Everyone took their turn to use the bathroom. The boys who worked downstairs in the warehouse arrived by 8.30 am. They knew nothing about the hiding-place so everybody in the annexe had to have finished washing by then as sounds of running water would make the workers suspicious.

A breakfast of bread and coffee was eaten at 9.00 am, in the van Daans' room, on the top floor, where any noise was least likely to be heard. For the same reason it was essential for everyone to sit as still as possible for the rest of the morning. Slippers, not shoes, were worn by anyone needing to move.

Anne and her books, before she was confined to the annexe. Mr Frank made sure that Anne, Margot and Peter tried to keep up with the school work they were missing. Anne liked learning, especially history, but hated mathematics.

AFTERNOON

The warehouse boys went for lunch at 12.30 pm, so the hiders could move around freely until they came back at 2.00 pm. During the lunch break the helpers from the office below would come up for a bowl of soup and listen to BBC news. The rest of the working day was spent sleeping, reading, writing or helping with office paperwork. Anne learned to write in shorthand.

EVENING

After the office and warehouse closed it was possible to move around again. Anne got some exercise by practising ballet steps. The evening meal, consisting mainly of vegetables, was prepared and eaten. Housework and washing could be done without worrying about the noise of running water or furniture being moved. After listening to the BBC again, it would be time to take turns in the bathroom and get ready for bed. As the youngest, Anne went first.

Weekends

The office and warehouse were closed at weekends, so there was no risk of attracting the attention of workers downstairs. But, just because the building was supposed to be quite empty, it was even more important not to make the slightest noise that might attract a nosy neighbour or a passing policeman. For the same reason it was impossible to put out bags of rubbish or food leftovers. Everything had to be burned in the stove, after dark – even in the hottest weather.

Food

Feeding eight people was a continuing problem for their helpers, who had to buy forged **ration cards**. Miep shopped every day, helped by a friendly greengrocer who never asked why she was buying so much more than she and her husband could ever eat. The greengrocer even delivered sacks of potatoes to the Prinsengracht office so that she did not have to wheel them through the streets on her bicycle, and risk being stopped by a curious policeman or soldier. It was Peter van Daan's job to haul heavy shopping up from the ground floor to the attic where it could be stored. Mrs van Daan did most of the cooking, with Margot and Anne helping with chores like cleaning vegetables. When they were lucky enough to get fresh meat Mr van Daan used his expert knowledge of spices to make tasty sausages as a treat.

Presents and Panics

It was a daily challenge for everyone in the annexe to be cheerful and co-operative and keep boredom at bay. In winter it was too dark to read after four in the afternoon. In summer it was impossible to escape the heat by going outside to feel the breeze and smell the flowers. Anne noted in her diary,

The helpers – Miep Gies (seated) and Elli Vossen who both worked for Mr Frank.

'We while away the time with all kinds of crazy activities; telling riddles, doing **callisthenics** in the dark, speaking English or French, reviewing books – after a while everything gets boring.'
(28 November 1942, p74)

Worst of all was the sense of complete imprisonment and not being able to do the most normal things, like walk in a park, ride a bicycle or even sit out in a garden. At weekends it was necessary to sit behind closed curtains.

Treats and festivals

Everyone had something they particularly missed – for Margot, a hot bath, for Peter, the cinema, and for Mrs van Daan, cream cakes.

A special Christmas page (27 December 1943) from Anne's diary. She decorated it with pictures cut out from cards and papers.

The helpers brought in regular supplies of books to help pass the time. Whenever possible the hiders tried to mark special occasions, like Jewish religious festivals and Dutch national days. On Peter's 16th birthday he got a game of Monopoly and, to show that he was now a grown-up, a razor. On her 15th birthday Anne got four books, two bunches of flowers, jam, gingerbread, yoghurt, cheese, a bracelet, a handkerchief and a set of underwear.

The tower of the Westerkerk church could be seen from the front attic window. Its quarter hour chime was a constant reminder of the slow passing of the hours.

WHO'S THAT?

One evening, around eight o'clock, when everyone working downstairs had gone home, a doorbell suddenly rang loudly. Everyone froze. Had someone seen a chink of light or heard a noise? Was it the police? Or a German patrol? They waited. Nothing happened. Whoever it was simply went away.

One night Mrs van Daan was sure she could hear a burglar overhead, in the attic. Peter went up with a torch to investigate – and found himself facing a horde of rats! There was a quick and easy answer to the problem. Peter's pet cat, Mouschi, was set on guard there from then onwards.

Burglars

Just over a year after the Franks moved into the secret annexe, the Prinsengracht building was burgled. One Thursday night thieves forced their way in with a crowbar. Anne noted their haul in her diary: '… two cash boxes containing 40 guilders, blank cheque books and, worst of all, coupons for 320 pounds of sugar.' (16 July 1943, p114)

Another burglary occurred in March 1944. Once again the hiders wondered whether the intruders had heard them or noticed anything suspicious. But nothing came of it.

A third break-in took place on Sunday 9 April, 1944. This was much more frightening. The four men went downstairs. Mr van Daan tried a bold bluff and shouted 'Police!'. The burglars ran off and the men came back upstairs. But because the street door had been broken right down a neighbour sent for the police. Naturally they searched the building:

'… a noise below… Footsteps in the house, the private office, the kitchen, then… on the staircase. All sounds of breathing stopped, eight hearts pounded… then a rattling at the bookcase… then we heard a tin fall, and the footsteps receded… I heard several sets of teeth chattering, no-one said a word.'   (11 April 1944, p253)

THE WAR GOES ON

When Mr Dussel joined the hiders in November 1942 he brought them up to date with what had been happening to other Dutch Jews. Anne recorded in her diary with horror,

'… night after night, green and grey military vehicles cruise the streets. They knock on every door, asking whether any Jews live there. If so, the whole family is immediately taken away… It's impossible to escape their clutches unless you go into hiding… No-one is spared… all are marched to their death.'

(19 November 1942, pp72–73)

TURNING THE TIDE

From the outbreak of war in 1939, right up to the time the Franks went into hiding in July 1942, the armies of **Nazi** Germany seemed unbeatable. But from 1943 onwards the fighting began to go against them. Every night British and American bombers flew over Amsterdam on their way to targets in Germany. Anne was terrified by the anti-aircraft fire sent up at them.

'I crawl into Father's bed nearly every night for comfort.. I know it sounds childish but wait till it happens to you! The ack-ack guns make so much noise you can't hear your own voice.'

(10 March 1943, p89)

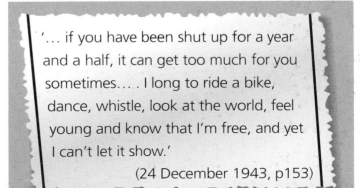

Destroyed! A registration office, where records about people were kept, is blown up by the Dutch resistance. Without accurate information about individuals – their age, appearance, address and workplace – it would be impossible to know who was on the run or in hiding.

In July 1943 Anne noted in her diary that the British had landed in Sicily. Mr Frank hoped this would be a turning point. The surrender of Italy, Germany's ally, in September 1943 made him hope that the war might even end that year.

On Christmas Eve that year Anne confided to her diary her feelings of frustration,

'… if you have been shut up for a year and a half, it can get too much for you sometimes…. I long to ride a bike, dance, whistle, look at the world, feel young and know that I'm free, and yet I can't let it show.'

(24 December 1943, p153)

The food in the
annexe was very
plain. Each person's
share was
measured carefully.

A SETBACK ON THE KITCHEN FRONT

On 14 March 1944 Anne recorded in her diary that
the **resistance** workers who supplied them with
forged **ration coupons** had been caught. The
hiders would have to make do with an even more
boring diet than they had already been living on,

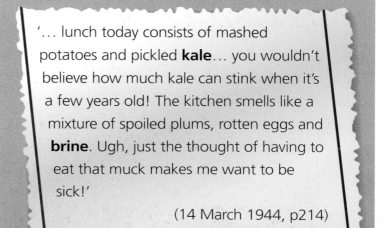

'… lunch today consists of mashed
potatoes and pickled **kale**… you wouldn't
believe how much kale can stink when it's
a few years old! The kitchen smells like a
mixture of spoiled plums, rotten eggs and
brine. Ugh, just the thought of having to
eat that muck makes me want to be
sick!'

(14 March 1944, p214)

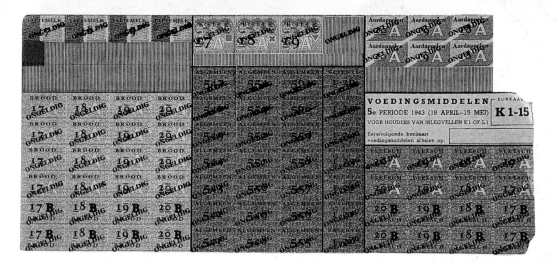

As the people in hiding did not officially exist they had to rely on their helpers to buy forged coupons for food rations.

INVASION!

On 6 June 1944 Anne recorded landings in northern France by **Allied** forces – American, British, Canadian and soldiers who had escaped from conquered countries, such as France and Poland.

The Allied troops met stiff resistance from the German armies occupying France, but by September 1944 British troops had driven them out of the south of the Netherlands. For the hiders in the annexe, however, liberation came too late.

'Will this year, 1944, bring us victory? We don't know yet. But where there's hope, there's life. It fills us with fresh courage and makes us strong again… It's now a matter of remaining calm and steadfast, of gritting our teeth and keeping a stiff upper lip!… Oh, Kitty, the best part about the invasion is that I have the feeling that friends are on the way.'

(6 June 1944, p309)

ARREST

The last entry in Anne's diary is dated Tuesday 1 August 1944 – over two years after the Franks had gone into hiding. On the morning of Friday 4 August Otto Frank went to Peter's room as usual to give him an English lesson. Just as they were about to start they heard angry voices downstairs. A few minutes later they could hear a scraping noise as the bookcase disguising the entrance to the secret annexe was pulled back.

Five men with guns, one a German policeman, burst in. The German, Karl Silberbauer, shouted for them to hand over any valuables they had. Grabbing a briefcase, he threw its contents – including Anne's diary – onto the floor and used it to carry away money and jewellery belonging to the people in the annexe. All eight of them were arrested and hustled away to German police headquarters.

Last journey. A list of passengers on the last train from Westerbork to Auschwitz contains the names of the Frank family. Mr Frank is listed as a trader, the others as having no occupation.

	5		5 September		4	Blatt
			JUDENTRANSPORT AUS DEN NIEDERLANDEN – LAGER WESTERBORK			
			Haeftlinge			
301.	✓Engers		Isidor — ✓30.4.	93 –	Kaufmann	
302	✓ Engers		Leonard	15.6. 20 –	Lamdarbeiter	
303	✓ Franco		Manfred – ✓1.5.	05 –	Verleger	
304.	Frank		Arthur	22.8. 81	Kaufmann	
305.	Frank ×		Isaac	✓29.11.87	Installateur	
306.	Frank		Margot	16.2. 26	ohne	
307.	Frank	✓	Otto	✓12.5. 89	Kaufmann	
308.	✓ Frank-Hollaender		Edith	16.1. 00	ohne	
309.	Frank		Anneliese	12.6. 29	ohne	
310.	v.Franck		Sara —	27.4. 02 –	Typistin	
311.	Franken		Rozanna	16.5. 96 –	Landarbeiter	
312.	✓ Franken-Weyand		Johanna	24.12.96 ▸	Landbauer	
313.	Franken		Hermann — ✓12.5.34		ohne	
314.	Franken		Louis	10.8. 17 –	Gaertner	

Waiting to go. Jews gathered in Amsterdam to leave for Westerbork concentration camp.

BETRAYED

By the autumn of 1944, out of a population of 9,000,000 some 300,000 Dutch people had been forced to go and work in Germany. Another 250,000 had gone into hiding to avoid this. Almost 20,000 were being held in camps as prisoners of war or because of their political beliefs.

About 25,000 Dutch Jews had gone into hiding. For some, like the people in the annexe, this meant living in attics, or back rooms or even under the floorboards of a house or barn. In the countryside, however, small children could often be passed off as relatives, sent out from the cities to keep them safe from bombing. Of the Dutch Jews who hid, 16,000 survived the war but 9000 were either discovered by chance raids or betrayed by **informers**.

Round-up.
German troops
on patrol found
and arrested
Jews in hiding.

People betrayed the Jews for money or because they were Dutch **Nazis** who supported German **persecution** of Jews. The usual payment to an **informer** amounted to about one week's average wages. But sometimes betrayal was caused by threats of arrest or torture. Who betrayed the secret of 263 Prinsengracht, or why, has never been definitely established. A house overlooking the back of the hide-out was occupied by Dutch Nazis who may have noticed lights or movement in the rooms that were supposed to be empty.

SEPARATED

The eight people in the annexe were allowed to pack a few clothes. Their two helpers, Mr Koophuis and Mr Kraler, were also arrested and sent to a separate prison camp. Both survived. On the day of the arrests, after work was over, Miep, her husband Jan, and other members of staff went up to the annexe and rescued Anne's diary, the Frank family photo album and other books and papers.

Westerbork – the Dutch concentration camp where Jews were crowded into flimsy wooden huts.

A week later the secret annexe was emptied of everything else on German orders.

Four days after their arrest, the people from the annexe were sent to Westerbork for the rest of August. On 3 September they were loaded onto the last train out of the camp and crammed into a boxcar with 70 others, headed for Auschwitz **concentration camp** in Poland. When they got there two days later the men and the women were separated from one another. The old, sick and under-fifteens – who were judged too weak even for slave labour – were sent to be executed in the gas chambers the very next day. Anne was just fifteen and so she was sent to the nearby women's camp at Birkenau, along with her sister and mother and Mrs van Daan. It was the last time she saw her adored father.

Starvation and Liberation

Strike!

In September 1944 the Dutch government in London ordered Dutch railwaymen to strike so that German forces could not move supplies around the Netherlands. The **resistance** groups added to the chaos by blowing up railway lines. The Germans hit back by carrying off livestock, food supplies, machinery and even bicycles to Germany. They also stopped the movement of all food and fuel from the countryside into the cities. City-dwellers were forced to burn the woodwork of their homes to keep warm. Everything that could be eaten was eaten – even tulip bulbs. Even so 22,000 people died of hunger and cold. Many more were only saved from death by British airdrops in the weeks leading up to final **liberation** in May 1945.

Food from the sky. British planes drop emergency supplies to the starving Dutch in April 1945.

CAMP CONDITIONS

The camps at Auschwitz-Birkenau were built for mass-murder, either by gassing in specially built death chambers or by working people to death. Prisoners were given hardly anything to eat, and were herded together in unheated, crowded, filthy conditions. They could be tortured or beaten to death by their guards for the slightest offence – or sometimes no offence at all. Hundreds died daily for lack of food or medical attention. Camps in Germany itself were not equipped with gas-chambers but the neglect and ill-treatment of inmates was just as awful.

As the **Allies** closed in, officials in charge of many camps tried to dismantle them and move their prisoners out to hide the evidence of their crimes. No-one knows exactly how many died at Auschwitz-Birkenau – at least a million, or perhaps more than three times as many. There were 7600 left by the time the Russians liberated the camp on 27 January 1945. The remaining survivors had been moved on to other camps still under **Nazi** control.

SOLE SURVIVOR

Of the eight arrested in the annexe only Otto Frank survived the war. Mr van Daan was gassed a couple of weeks after arriving in Auschwitz. Mr Frank saw him being marched away to his death.

Peter van Daan was transferred to the camp at Mauthausen in Austria, where he died three days before the Americans liberated it. Mr Dussel was sent to Neuengamme in northern Germany, where he also died, in December 1944.

Anne's mother was so weak she died in Birkenau on 6 January, three weeks before the camp was liberated by the Russians. Margot, Anne and Mrs van Daan were moved to Bergen-Belsen camp in Germany in October 1944. Mrs van Daan was then sent on to Buchenwald, also in Germany, and finally to Theresienstadt in Czechoslovakia, where she died in the spring of 1945. Some time in February or March 1945 Margot caught typhus and died. Anne was left completely alone. Lies Goosen, an old school friend of Anne's, was able to talk to her briefly through a barbed wire fence,

Many who did survive the camps, like Otto Frank, lost all their family.

'She immediately began to cry, and she told me, "I don't have any parents any more" … I always think, if Anne had known that her father was still alive, she might have had more strength … .'

Another eyewitness said that Anne was so disgusted by the lice and fleas in her clothes that she had thrown them away and just wrapped herself in a blanket, even though it was winter. Later in March Anne, too, died of typhus. The camp was liberated by British soldiers a month later.

After being freed from Auschwitz, Mr Frank searched Birkenau but found no trace of his wife or daughters. By 3 June he had made his way back, by way of Russia and France, to Amsterdam and 263 Prinsengracht. Two months later a letter came from someone who had been in Belsen and could confirm personally that Margot and Anne had died there.

Survivors. Prisoners liberated at Dachau concentration camp.

THE DIARY

In March 1944 Anne Frank heard a Dutch broadcaster from London say that after the war the government ought to make an official collection of letters and diaries to record what the nation had been through. Anne excitedly wrote in her diary,

> 'Just imagine how interesting it would be if I were to publish a novel about the Secret Annexe. The title alone would make people think it was a detective story.'　　　(29 March 1944, p242)

A few days later she wrote

> 'When I write I can shake off all my cares ... But ... will I ever be able to write anything great, will I ever become a journalist or a writer? I hope so, oh, I hope so very much.'
> 　　　　　　　　　　　(5 April 1944, p248)

A month after that she declared her firm intention that,

> '... after the war I'd like to publish a book called 'The Secret Annexe'. It remains to be seen whether I'll succeed but my diary can serve as the basis.'　(11 May 1944, p292)

PUBLICATION

When Miep Gies gave Anne's diary to Otto Frank he was astonished that his daughter had described daily life in the annexe so well. He translated sections into German so that his mother could read them. After he had let other people read parts of the diary a newspaper article appeared praising it. In 1947 a publisher put out a small edition of 1500 copies. It soon sold out, as did a second printing. It was translated into French and German. An English version appeared in 1951. In 1956 the diary became a play, and a film in 1959. In 1960, 263 Prinsengracht was opened as a museum – 600,000 people visit it each year. Since its first publication, Anne's diary has been translated into 50 languages and over 20,000,000 copies have been sold.

Anne's original tartan-covered diary lies alongside a scrapbook and exercise books for schoolwork and writing stories.

The diary — or diaries?

After Anne decided that her diary might be published one day she set about revising it. The original entries were copied out on to single sheets of paper. Some sections were rewritten, some cut out altogether and some added. The revisions stopped at 24 March 1944.

Miep Gies passed both the original diary and the revised single sheets to Otto Frank. His edition of *Het Achterhuis* (*The Annexe*) drew on both versions but also left out passages he thought unimportant, uninteresting or embarrassing. He also disguised the names of the hiders and helpers, as Anne had, so that their privacy would be protected if the book were ever published.

The diary names are as follows:-

Diary Name	Real Name
Mr Koophuis	Johannes Kleiman
Mr Kraler	Victor Kugler
Elli Vossen	Bep Voskuijl
Mr Vossen	Mr Voskuijl
Miep van Santen	Miep Gies (originally Miep Santrouschitz)
Henk van Santen	Jan Gies
The van Daan family	The van Pels family
Albert Dussel	Fritz Pfeffer

TRUE OR FALSE?

From the 1950s onwards a number of critics began to question whether Anne Frank's diary was genuine. Some insisted that it must be a fake because it was simply too well written to have been produced by a girl of 15. After Otto Frank's death in 1980 he left all Anne's original writings to the government of the Netherlands. They were submitted to careful examination by experts on paper, ink and handwriting and proved to be entirely genuine.

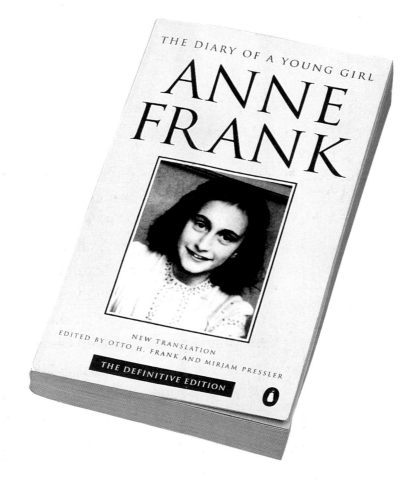

THE DIARY OF A YOUNG GIRL

ANNE FRANK

NEW TRANSLATION
EDITED BY OTTO H. FRANK AND MIRJAM PRESSLER

THE DEFINITIVE EDITION

WHAT PEOPLE THINK ABOUT ANNE FRANK'S DIARY

'I hope I shall be able to confide in you completely, as I have never been able to do in anyone before, and I hope that you will be a great support and comfort to me.'
Anne Frank – first diary entry, 12 June 1942

'Anne's diary tells a story that is true, memorable, important and strongly personalized … compelling reading.'
Rabbi Julia Neuberger, 1995

'By coincidence I came across a diary that was written during the war. The Netherlands State Institute for War Documentation already has about 200 such diaries, but it would surprise me if there was another one which was as pure, as intelligent and yet as human as this one.'
Professor Jan Romein, historian, 1946

'The Diary … remains astonishing and excruciating … evidence of her ferocious appetite for life. It gnaws at us still.'
The New York Times Book Review, 1995

'From time to time she talks about the horrors beyond her window, but most of the diary is about the turmoil within her growing heart. Cooped up, misunderstood, she is every teenager … she spends her time trying to figure out who will love her as she is and how she will make do with last year's undervests.'
Anna Quindlen, writer, 1994

'I'm told that every night when the sun goes down, somewhere in the world the curtain is going up on the stage play made from Anne's diary…. her voice has reached the far edges of the earth.'

Miep Gies, helper of the Frank family, 1987

'Anne never spoke about hatred anywhere in her diary. She wrote that despite everything, she believed in the goodness of people. And that when the war was over, she wanted to work for the world and for people. This is the duty I have taken over from her. I have received many thousands of letters. Young people especially always want to know how these terrible things could ever have happened. I answer them as well as I can, and I often finish by saying : "I hope that Anne's book will have an effect on the rest of your life so that … you will work for unity and peace."'

Otto Frank, father of Anne Frank, 1970

'People throughout the world have read Anne's diary and, because it captured so well the feelings and experiences of one of the war's many victims, have made Anne Frank a symbol of the millions of Jews who perished in the Second World War. Moreover, Anne has become a symbol for all people who are persecuted today for their background, the colour of their skin, or their beliefs.'

Ruud van der Rol and Rian Verhoeven,
Anne Frank House, 1994

ANNE FRANK — TIMELINE

1889 Otto Frank is born in Frankfurt–am–Main, Germany

1900 Edith Hollander is born in Aachen, Germany

1914 Outbreak of the First World War

1918 (11 November) World War One ends

1919 National Socialist German Workers' Party (**Nazi** party) founded
Versailles Treaty signed

1925 Otto Frank marries Edith Hollander. They settle in Otto's
mother's house in Frankfurt

1926 (16 November) Margot Frank born

1927 The Frank family move to a new home at 307 Marbachweg

1929 Business crisis in USA and Europe causes trade collapse and mass
unemployment
(12 June) Anne Frank born

1931 Collapse of German banking system.
The Frank family move to 24 Ganghoferstrasse

1933 (30 January) Hitler becomes Chancellor of Germany
Enabling Law grants Hitler the powers of a **dictator** for four years
Otto Frank moves to Amsterdam. The rest of the family go to
Aachen, Germany.
Edith and Margot join Otto in December.

1934 Anne joins her family in Amsterdam in February and goes to
Montessori school

1935 Anti-Jewish Nuremberg Laws proclaimed

1936 Olympic Games held in Berlin

1938 Germany takes over Austria and the Sudetenland

1939 Germany takes over Bohemia and Moravia and conquers Poland
(3 September) Britain and France declare war on Germany

1940 Otto Frank's business moves to 263 Prinsengracht
(10 May) Germany invades the Netherlands
(14 May) Dutch forces surrender

1941 Otto Frank's Opekta–Works changes its name to Trading
Company Gies & Co.
(September) Margot and Anne Frank transferred to Jewish school
(11 December) Germany invades the Soviet Union and declares
war on the U.S.A.

1942 (12 June) Anne receives a diary as a birthday present

(6 July) Frank family go into hiding

(13 July) van Daan (Van Pels) family join the Frank family in the annexe

(16 November) Albert Dussel (Fritz Pfeffer) moves into the annexe

1943 German army attacking Stalingrad surrenders.

Italy surrenders to the Allies

1944 (6 June) Allies invade Normandy

(12 June) Hitler launches V bombing campaign against Britain

(20 July) Hitler survives an attempt to kill him

(4 August) People hiding in the annexe are arrested and

(8 August) transported to Westerbork and

(3 September) then to Auschwitz

(11 September) Allied troops reach the borders of Germany

(September) Allied troops free the southern Netherlands

(October) Anne and Margot are transferred to Bergen-Belsen

1945 (27 January) Auschwitz is liberated by the Russian army

(March) Anne and Margot die

(30 April) Hitler kills himself in Berlin

(5 May) **Liberation** of the Netherlands

(8 May) VE (Victory in Europe) Day marks the end of the war in Europe

(3 June) Otto Frank returns to 263 Prinsengracht

1947 Diary published as *The Annexe* (*Het Achterhuis*) in Dutch

1951 Diary published in English

1952 Otto Frank moves to Basel, Switzerland

1953 Otto Frank re-marries

1956 Anne Frank's Diary is dramatized as a stage play

1957 Anne Frank Foundation established to manage 263 Prinsengracht as a museum

1959 Anne Frank's diary is filmed

1960 263 Prinsengracht opened as a museum

1980 Otto Frank dies

GLOSSARY

Allies countries united against an enemy

Aryan member of the highest racial group in the **Nazi** pyramid of human types. The word originally described a group of languages spoken in northern India from which both German and English have developed. Later the word meant people who spoke those languages. They were thought of as an ancient race of tough warriors of great beauty and high intelligence.

The language link is a matter of history. The idea of a heroic 'master race' has no basis.

brine salt water

callisthenics exercises

communists people who believe in a government based on the idea that a single ruling political party can run a country for all its people's benefit better than if they are left to make their own decisions and keep their own private homes, land and businesses. In practice communist governments have usually been cruel dictatorships.

concentration camp a prison where political opponents could be concentrated together; in theory they were to be 'educated' through work and exercise; in practice torture was common

dictator ruler with complete power, not answerable to a parliament

informers people who supply secret information for money

kale cabbage

liberation setting free

Nazi short name of the National Socialist German Workers' Party (*Nationalsozialistische Deutsche Arbeiterpartei*), led by Adolf Hitler. The Nazis ruled Germany 1933–1945.

neutral not taking sides

pension boarding house

persecution deliberate ill-treatment

ration cards/coupons documents allowing the holder to buy a limited amount of food or goods

rationing official system of sharing out limited supplies of food

resistance fighting back. The Dutch resistance movement fought against occupation by the Nazis.

SA (*Sturmabteilungen*; Stormtroopers) private army of the Nazi party

swastika (*Hakenkreuz*) official symbol of Nazism; based on an Indian design, associated with the ancient Aryans

synagogue Jewish place of worship

unemployment not having work

INDEX